When Rain Falls

Written by **Melissa Stewart**

Illustrated by **Constance R. Bergum**

PEACHTREE
ATLANTA

For J. L. Bell, who introduced me to the
Society of Children's Book Writers and Illustrators

—*M. S.*

For my forever friends Kathy and Shelley

—*C. B.*

Published by
PEACHTREE PUBLISHERS
1700 Chattahoochee Avenue
Atlanta, Georgia 30318-2112
www.peachtree-online.com

Text © 2008 by Melissa Stewart
Illustrations © 2008 by Constance R. Bergum

Art direction by Loraine M. Joyner
Composition by Melanie McMahon Ives

Illustrations created in watercolor on 100% rag watercolor paper. Title typeset in ITC
Britannic Bold; text typeset in Baskerville Infant.

Printed in Singapore
10 9 8 7 6 5 4 3 2 1
First Edition

Library of Congress Cataloging-in-Publication Data

Stewart, Melissa.
  When rain falls / written by Melissa Stewart ; illustrated by Constance Bergum.-- 1st ed.
    p. cm.
  ISBN-13: 978-1-56145-438-9 / ISBN 10: 1-56145-438-9
  1. Rain and rainfall--Juvenile literature. 2. Animal behavior--Juvenile literature. I.
Bergum, Constance Rummel. II. Title.
  QC924.7S745 2008
  591.72'2--dc22
                2007031395

nside clouds, water droplets budge and bump, crash and clump. The drops grow larger and larger, heavier and heavier until they fall to the earth.

When rain falls in your neighborhood,

you run inside and wait for the storm to end.

When rain falls in a forest…

...scurrying squirrels suddenly stop. They pull their long, bushy tails over their heads like umbrellas.

A hawk puffs out its feathers to keep water out and warmth in.

Chickadees stay warm and dry inside their tree hole homes.

A doe and fawn take cover
under a leafy tree canopy.

A red fox family nestles
in a warm, cozy den.

When rain falls on a field…

...plump little caterpillars crawl under leaves and cling to stems. Adult butterflies dangle from brightly colored flower heads.

A raindrop knocks a ladybug off a slippery stem. The insect bounces into the air and then tumbles to the ground.

A spider watches and waits as the rain beats down on its carefully built web.

A mouse crouches under
a fallen leaf.

Bees hide in hives, and
ants stay safe in their
underground nests.

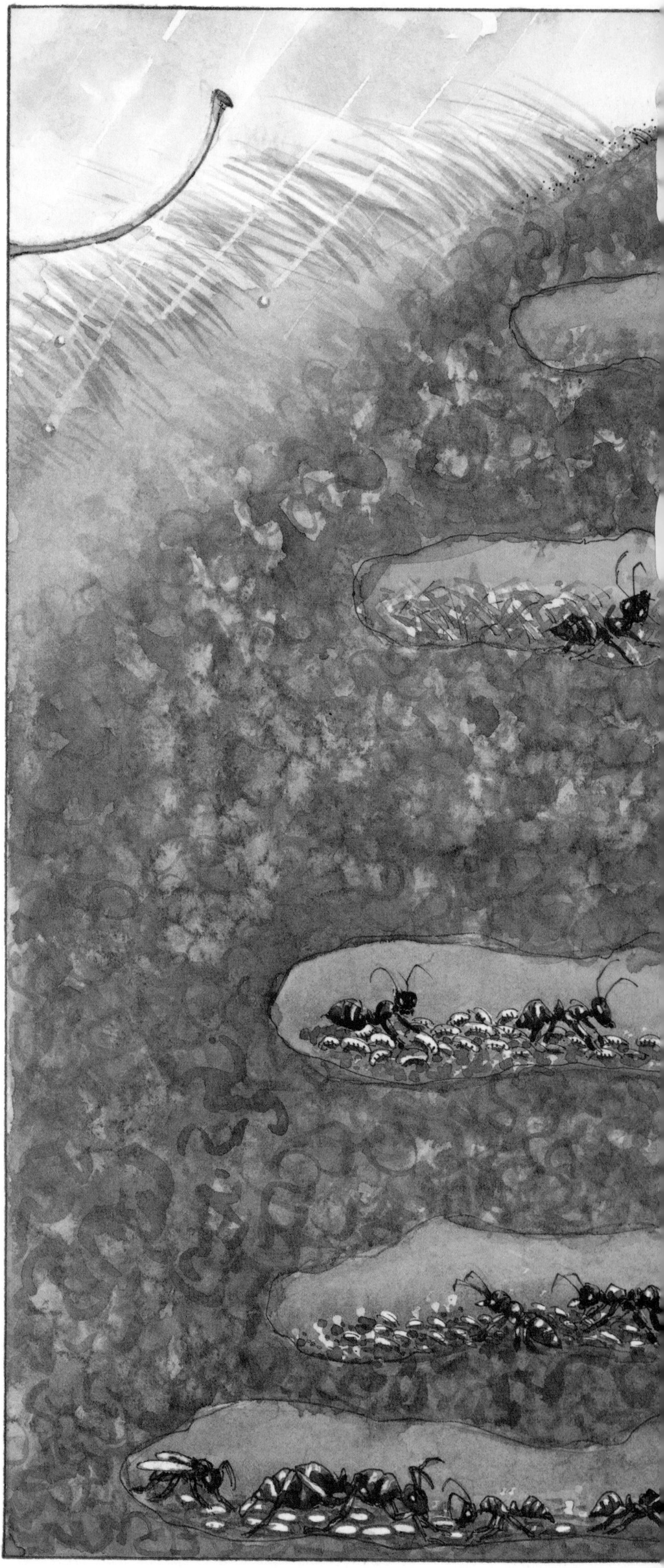

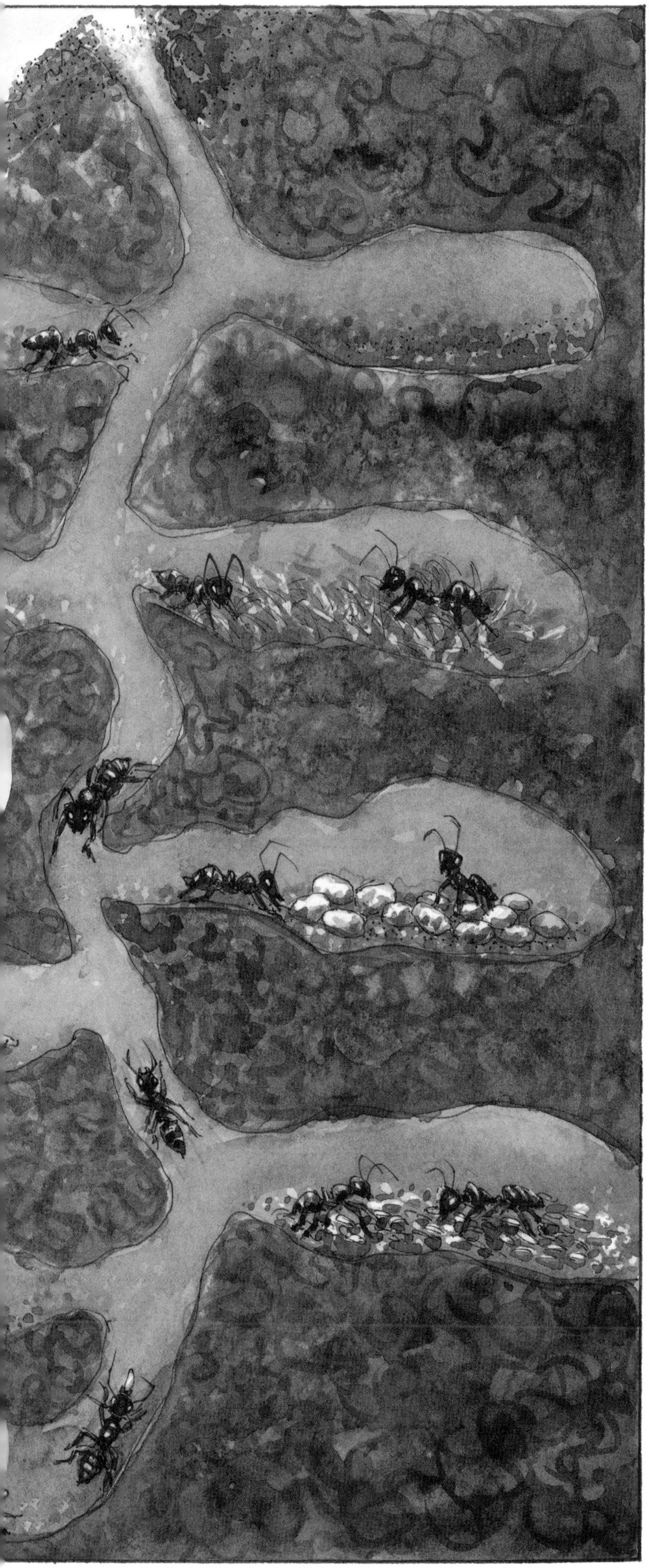

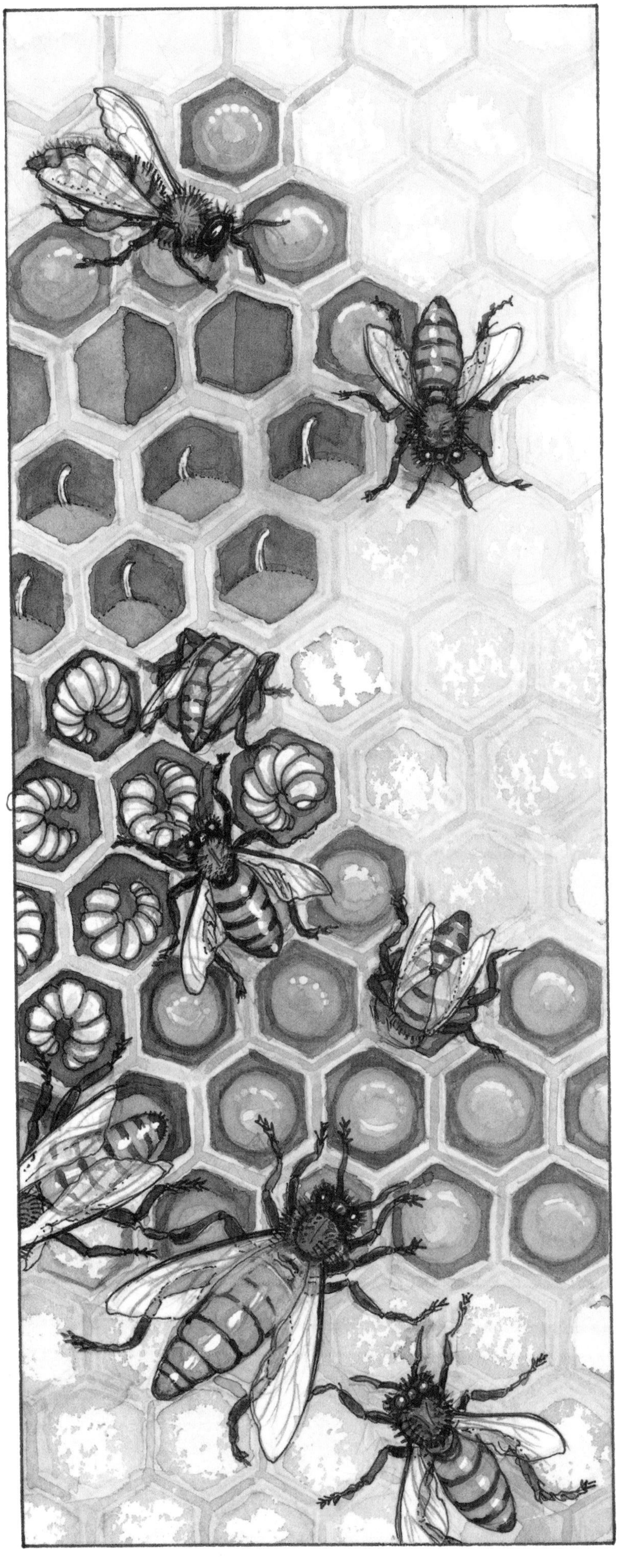

When rain falls in a wetland…

...turtles tuck in their tiny heads. Rain splatters against their hard, strong shells.

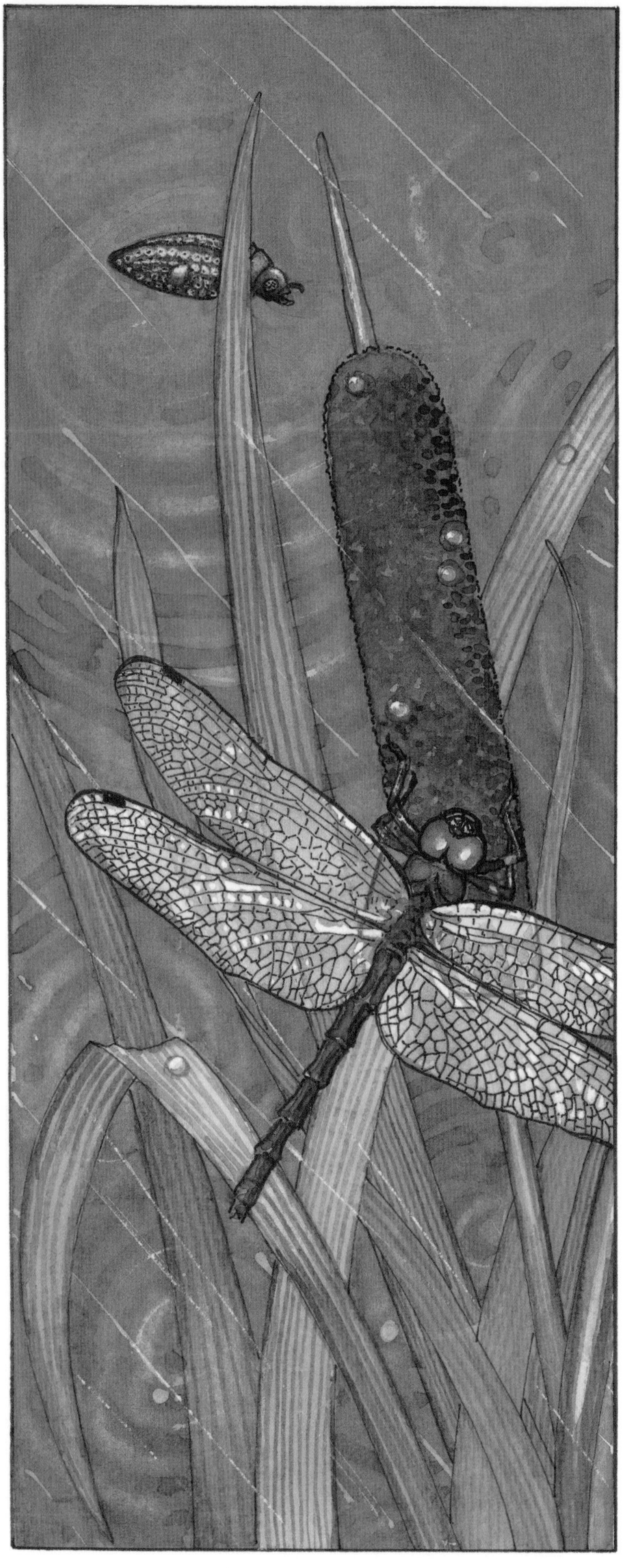
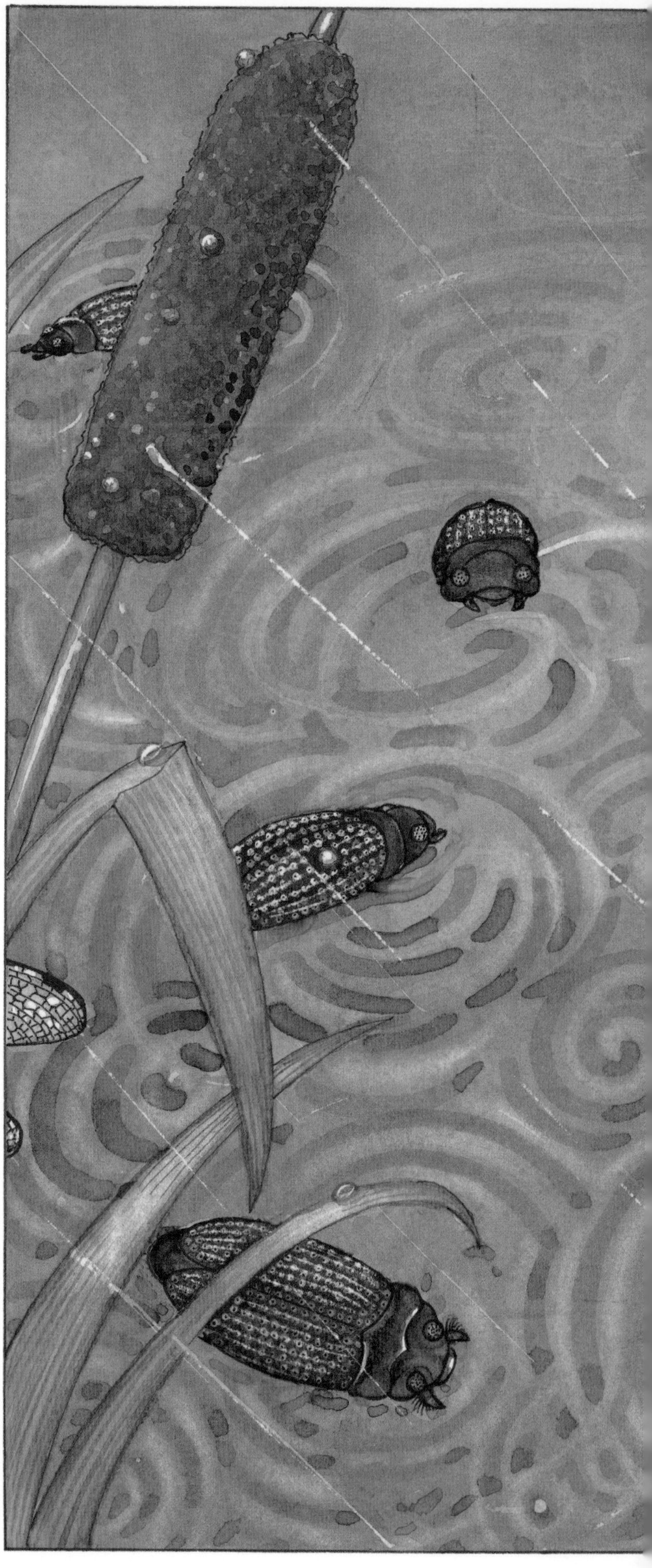

A dragonfly swoops down to perch
below a fluffy cattail seedhead.

Whirligig beetles swim in circles
and struggle to stay afloat.

Sparrows huddle deep inside
a dense cluster of leafy bushes.
But ducks continue to cruise
through the water. Raindrops
slide right off
their oily feathers.

*When rain falls
in a desert...*

…a rattlesnake squeezes into a rocky crevice. It curls up tight and falls asleep.

A tarantula scuttles into
an underground tunnel.

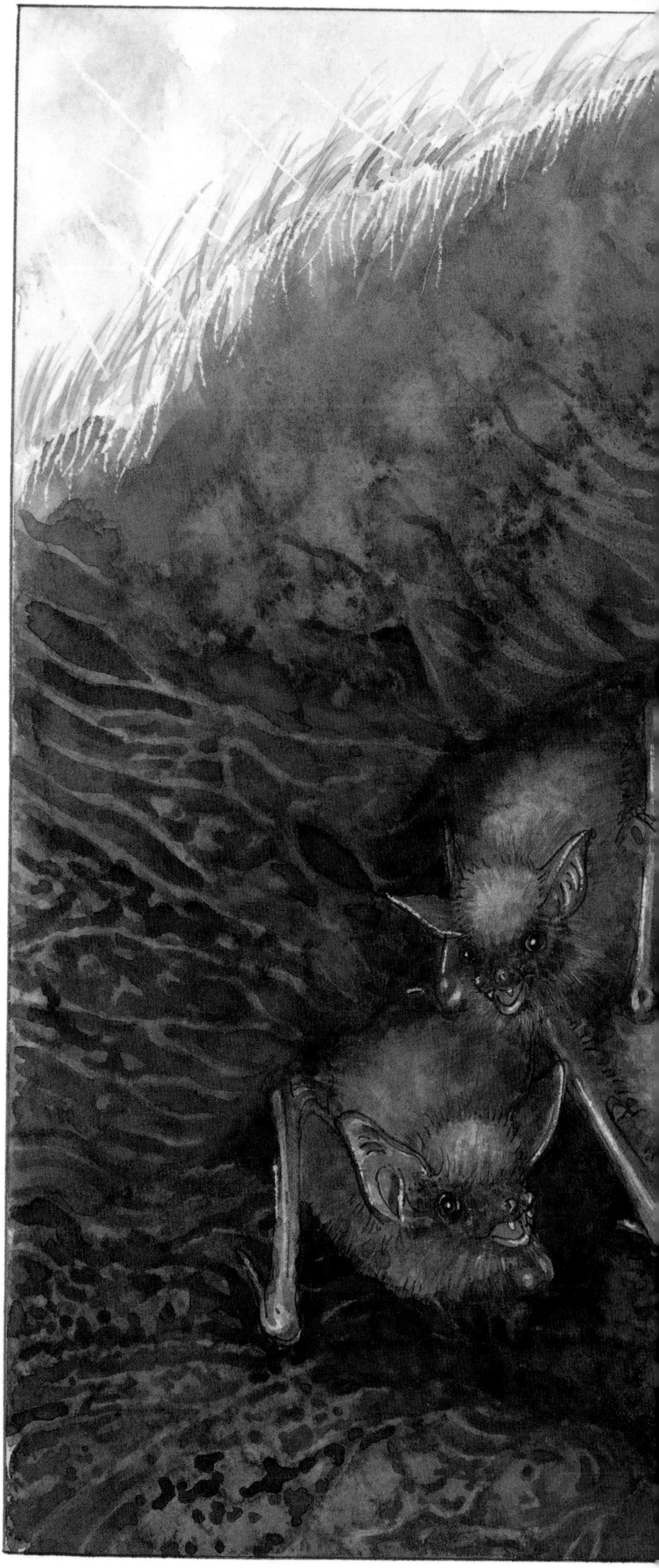

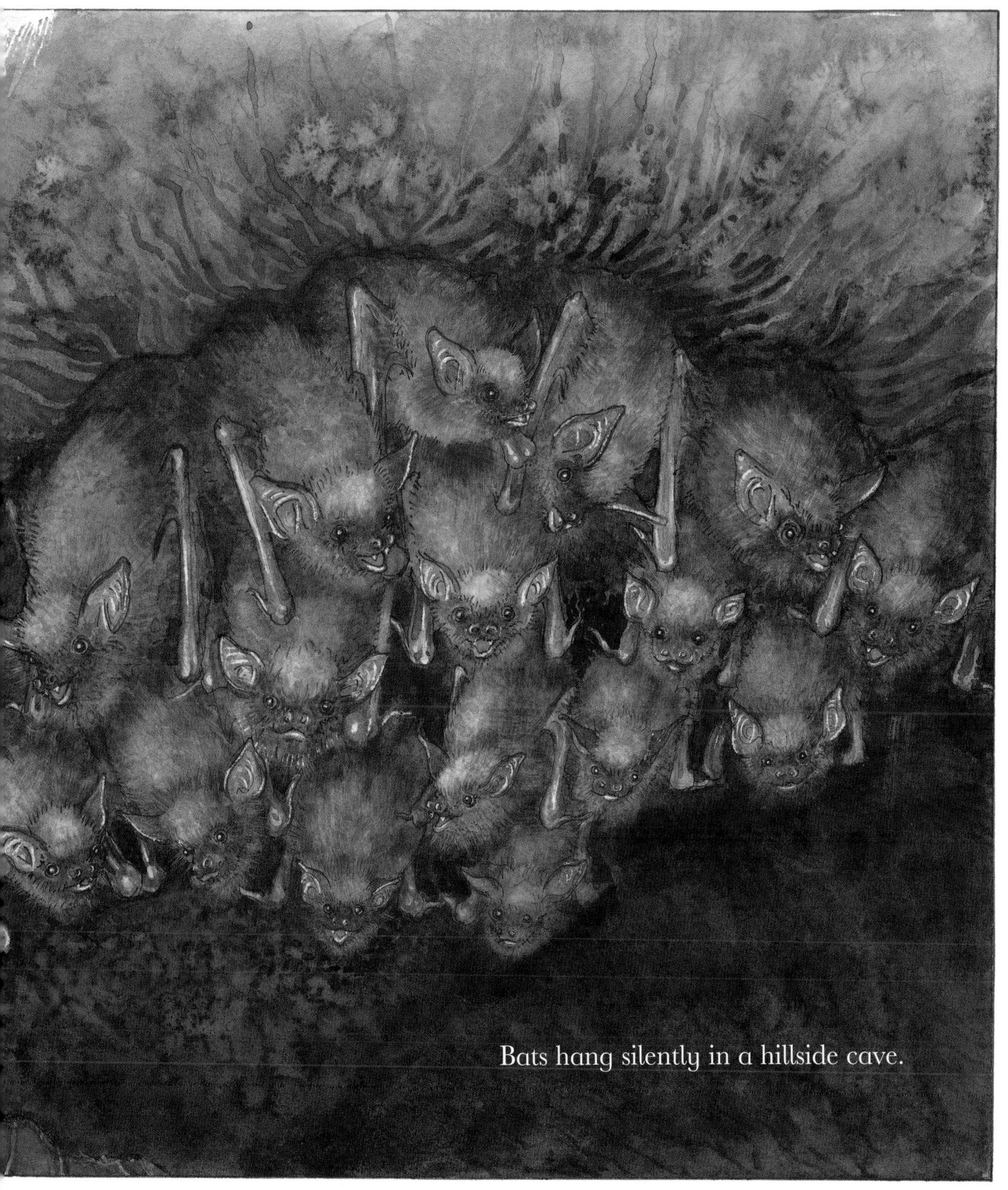

Bats hang silently in a hillside cave.

An elf owl
takes cover
in a cactus
nest.

Spadefoot toads dig to the surface. They mate, lay eggs, and then burrow back into the sand.

When the rain stops…

...animals living in fields and forests, wetlands
and deserts return to their daily routines.

And so do you.

4/08